A NOTE TO PARENTS

When your children are ready to "step into reading," giving them the right books is as crucial as giving them the right food to eat. **Step into Reading Books** present exciting stories and information reinforced with lively, colorful illustrations that make learning to read fun, satisfying, and worthwhile. They are priced so that acquiring an entire library of them is affordable. And they are beginning readers with a difference—they're written on five levels.

Early Step into Reading Books are designed for brand-new readers, with large type and only one or two lines of very simple text per page. **Step 1 Books** feature the same easy-to-read type as the Early Step into Reading Books, but with more words per page. **Step 2 Books** are both longer and slightly more difficult, while **Step 3 Books** introduce readers to paragraphs and fully developed plot lines. **Step 4 Books** offer exciting nonfiction for the increasingly independent reader.

The grade levels assigned to the five steps—preschool through kindergarten for the Early Books, preschool through grade 1 for Step 1, grades 1 through 3 for Step 2, grades 2 through 3 for Step 3, and grades 2 through 4 for Step 4—are intended only as guides. Some children move through all five steps very rapidly; others climb the steps over a period of several years. Either way, these books will help your child "step into reading" in style!

For Matt,
who likes chameleons, too
—M.K.

For Halim
—B.B.

Text copyright © 2001 by Michelle Knudsen.
Illustrations copyright © 2001 by Bryn Barnard.
All rights reserved under International and Pan-American Copyright Conventions.
Published in the United States by Random House, Inc., New York, and simultaneously
in Canada by Random House of Canada Limited, Toronto.

www.randomhouse.com/kids

Library of Congress Cataloging-in-Publication Data
Knudsen, Michelle.
Colorful chameleons! / Michelle Knudsen ; illustrated by Bryn Barnard.
p.   cm. — (Step into reading. Step 2)
ISBN 0-375-80665-2 (trade) — ISBN 0-375-90665-7 (lib. bdg.)
1. Chameleons—Juvenile literature. [1. Chameleons.] I. Barnard, Bryn, ill. II. Title.
III. Step into reading. Step 2 book.
QL666.L23 K68 2001
597.95'6—dc21
00-045700
Printed in the United States of America   June 2001   10 9 8 7 6 5 4 3 2 1

STEP INTO READING, RANDOM HOUSE, and the Random House colophon are registered trademarks
and the Step into Reading colophon is a trademark of Random House, Inc.

Step into Reading®

COLORFUL CHAMELEONS!*

By Michelle Knudsen   Illustrated by Bryn Barnard

A Step 2 Book

Random House 🏠 New York

A strange creature

peers out from the shadows.

It has big, round eyes

and pointy horns

and swirls of colored scales.

What is this mysterious beast?

Up close,

it looks like a dinosaur.

Or maybe a dragon!

5

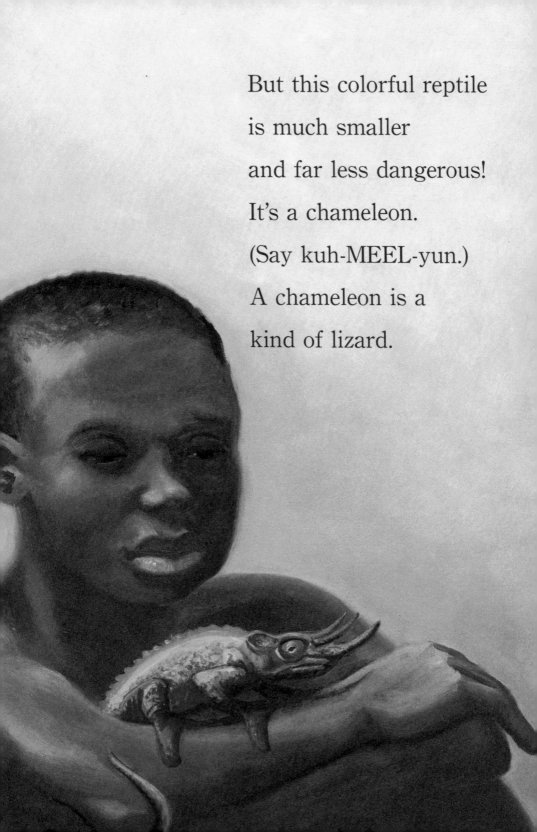

But this colorful reptile
is much smaller
and far less dangerous!
It's a chameleon.
(Say kuh-MEEL-yun.)
A chameleon is a
kind of lizard.

There are more than
one hundred species of
chameleons.
And even more
are still being discovered!

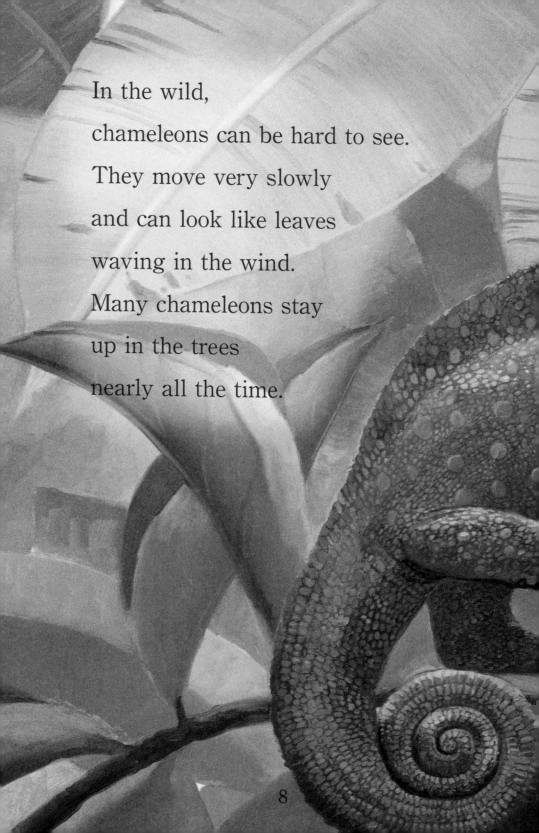

In the wild,
chameleons can be hard to see.
They move very slowly
and can look like leaves
waving in the wind.
Many chameleons stay
up in the trees
nearly all the time.

They only visit the
ground to lay eggs or
look for a mate.

Chameleons have
very special eyes.
Each eyeball
is covered by a dome
of scaly skin.
The chameleon sees through
a small hole in the center.

Both eyes can turn on their own
to look in any direction.
A chameleon can even look
in two directions
at once!

Many chameleons
have horns or crests.
Sometimes they use their horns
to push each other
during a fight.

Most chameleons have a
prehensile tail.
(Say pree-HEN-sil.)
This means they can use
their tails to grab things.

Chameleons' feet
are also good at grabbing.
They are shaped like V's.
This makes them perfect
for gripping branches.

Chameleons have a
special tongue
that helps them catch food.
It is very long
and has a sticky tip.

This chameleon is stalking a bug.
He turns both eyes
to look at his prey.
This tells him
how far away it is.

Next he slowly opens
his mouth.
Then—ZAP!
His tongue shoots out.
It sticks to the
unlucky bug.

The chameleon pulls his dinner
into his mouth.
He chews it up
with his tiny teeth.
Yum!

Most chameleons eat insects.

Many eat other things, too.

Some eat flowers, leaves,

or fruit.

Larger species sometimes eat
frogs, snails, small rodents,
birds, or other lizards.
Some kinds of chameleons
even hunt dangerous prey
like snakes and scorpions!

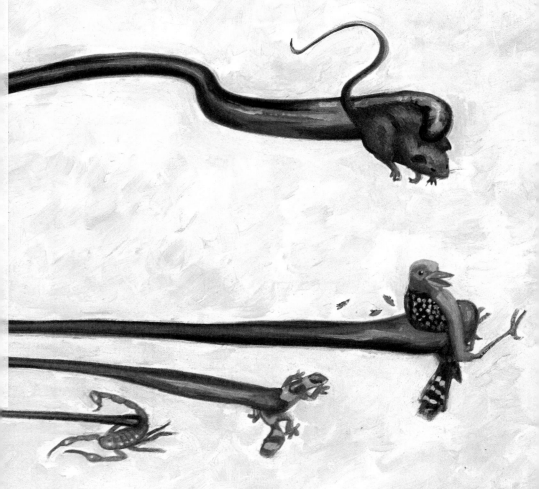

Chameleons are best known
for being able to change color.

Some people think chameleons
can change color
to match any background.
That's not true!

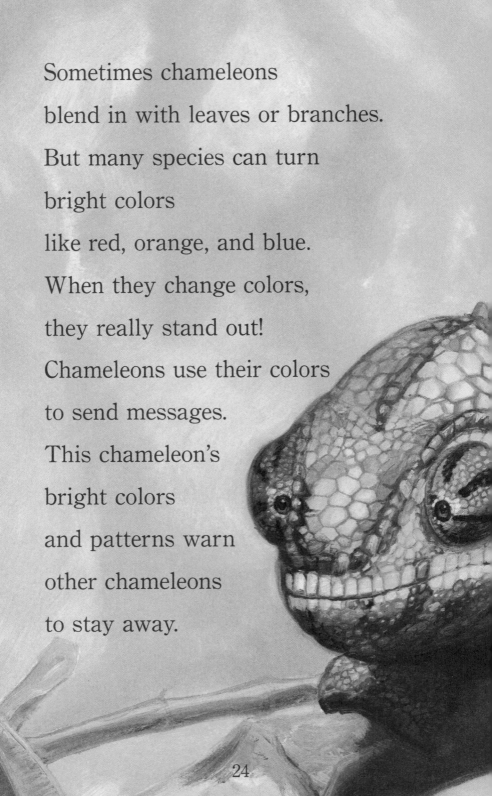

Sometimes chameleons
blend in with leaves or branches.
But many species can turn
bright colors
like red, orange, and blue.
When they change colors,
they really stand out!
Chameleons use their colors
to send messages.
This chameleon's
bright colors
and patterns warn
other chameleons
to stay away.

When chameleons fight,

they do not always attack.

They sometimes have a color contest!

Both chameleons

puff themselves up

and open their mouths wide.

They put on their best colors.
The one with the
fanciest colors or patterns
is the winner.
The loser runs away.

If chameleons
are hurt or afraid,
they turn darker and
show more complicated patterns.

Chameleons also use colors
to change their temperature.
They are cold-blooded animals.
This means their bodies
change temperature
with their environment.

When a chameleon
wants to warm up,
he moves into the sun.
Then he turns darker.
Dark colors help him soak up
more of the sun's heat.

This male chameleon
wants to attract a mate.
He bobs his head up and down
and from side to side.
This is how he says,
"I like you!"

If a female wants to mate,
she will display dull colors.
This female chameleon
does not want to mate.
Her colors are saying,
"Go away!"

Pregnant chameleons
are often the most colorful.

Some kinds of chameleons
give birth to live babies.
But most are egg-layers.
This female chameleon
is ready to lay her eggs.
She climbs down to the ground
and digs a nest.

She lays her eggs.
Then she buries them
under dirt and leaves.
Most chameleons lay
between thirty and sixty eggs
at one time.
Some can lay more than eighty!

Many months later, the eggs hatch.
Most baby chameleons have
dull colors.
This helps them hide
from predators.

Chameleons are only found
in certain areas of the world.
Almost all chameleons
live in Africa or
on an island called
Madagascar.
(Say ma-duh-GAS-ker.)

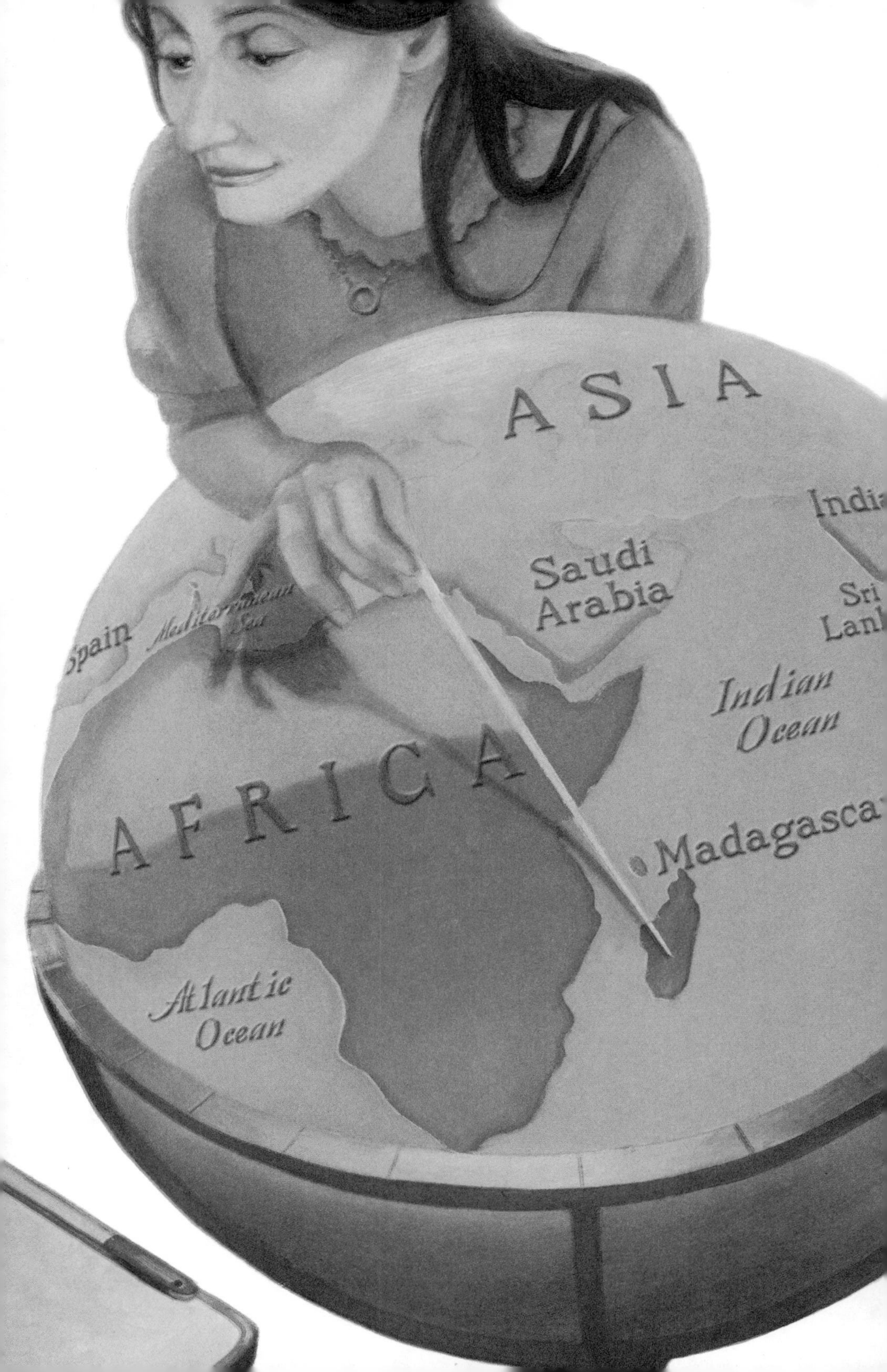
ASIA
Saudi Arabia
Spain
AFRICA
Indian Ocean
Atlantic Ocean

Each species of chameleon
likes a certain kind of habitat.
Some like rain forests.
Others like woods, mountains,
or grasslands.
A few even live in deserts.

Some chameleons can only live
in their special habitats.
If those places are destroyed,
the chameleons will not survive.

Some people raise
chameleons.
They want to help save
those chameleons
whose homes are being
destroyed.
But these reptiles
are very hard to raise.
Chameleons often don't
live very long
outside their
natural environment.

Pet stores sometimes
sell chameleons as pets.
They are beautiful creatures
and fun to look at.
But pet chameleons need
very special care
to stay happy and healthy.

These strange and colorful lizards
are probably happiest
in their special places
in the wild.